K I N D E R G A

Bible Songs and Finger Plays

Written by Carol Smith

Illustrated by Marilynn Barr

Cover Illustrated by Judy Hierstein

All rights reserved—Printed in the U.S.A.
Copyright © 2000 Shining Star Publications
A Division of Frank Schaffer Publications, Inc.
23740 Hawthorne Blvd., Torrance, CA 90505

Unless otherwise indicated, the New International Version of the Bible was used in preparing the activities in this book. Scripture taken from the HOLY BIBLE, NEW INTERNATIONAL VERSION. Copyright © 1973, 1978, 1984 International Bible Society. Used by permission of Zondervan Bible Publishers.

Table of Contents

To Teachers and Parents

Music and all of its components are powerful teaching tools that can be used to help children learn about God, His Word, and His teachings. This book is full of songs, marches, finger plays, and so much more children can sing and perform as they learn all about the elements of music: melody, rhythm, rhyme, movement, and performance. From finger puppet scripts to simple lyrics to the tunes of familiar children's songs, this book enables children to have a wonderful time practicing important skills as they learn about some valuable Christian concepts and many well-loved Bible stories.

There are four chapters in this book: Old Testament, New Testament, General Christian Concepts, and Prayers. The first two chapters deal with well-loved Bible stories and characters. The third chapter, General Christian Concepts, involves issues and ideas children will deal with all their lives—obedience, the church, joy, patience, kindness, goodness, gentleness, forgiveness, the Golden Rule, the fruit of the Spirit, faith, and love. The last chapter, Prayers, helps children learn to express their love for God and others.

Each chapter begins with a coloring page. Give each child a copy of this page and let the child color the picture, cut it out, and glue it onto black construction paper. Also featured throughout each chapter are many Bible verses and stories. Be sure to discuss these with the children.

These five components comprise each chapter: original songs, original lyrics to the tunes of familiar songs, finger plays, rhythm marches, and rhythm chants. They are described in detail on page 4.

Chapter Components

Original Songs

Each song is based on a Bible story, Bible passage, or Christian concept. Use the songs to summarize lessons based on these passages or concepts or during song time. The melody for each is included, and lyrics and motions are included separately (if motions accompany the song).

Original Lyrics to the Tunes of Familiar Songs

Since you are already familiar with these tunes, you can easily work them into your ongoing conversations with the children.

Finger Plays

Miniature plays are always fun for little fingers and are helpful in reminding children of important Bible stories and Christian concepts that will follow and guide them the rest of their lives. Patterns for puppets accompany some of the finger plays. For longer finger plays, the puppets (fingers) are listed first and then the script. Decide what works for your group, and make copies of the puppets for the children, if desired, so that each child has a set to use to re-enact the story.

Rhythm Marches

When it's time to get up and get moving, use these marches to reinforce some important Bible truths and to get some wiggles worked out. You can use the marches without a beat, but it always helps to have someone keep beat with a rhythm stick or small drum. Even a hand on a table or a simple metronome will work.

Rhythm Chants

It's always fun to gather in a circle and teach children a new rhythm, and these rhymes also feature good Biblical content. Each rhythm chant involves you and the children sitting on the floor (or in chairs) and making simple rhythms with your hands as you chant out an important Bible truth or Christian value.

All of the components in this book provide a great way for the children in your care to have a wonderful time learning about God and His Word. Smile, laugh, learn, and worship with these songs, finger plays, and rhythm activities!

The Old Testament

SS48843

Creation

(Genesis 1)

God Made It All

Teach the children this simple rhyme to help them learn all about God's beautiful creation. Keep in mind that children love repetition.

God made the world,
the earth, and the sky.

(Make the shape of the earth by placing tips of thumbs and fingers together.)

Then He made the animals
and birds that fly.

(Place thumbs side by side and move fingers together as wings.)

God made one man,
living all alone.

(Hold up index finger.)

Then He made a woman;
they made a home.

(Hold left index finger and then put the left and right index fingers together and join other fingers.)

With a "Moo, Moo," here,
And a "Moo, Moo," there,
Here a "Moo," there a "Moo,"
Everywhere a "Moo, Moo."
God made all the world we see.
Take a look around.

God Made All the World

Sing this song to the tune of "Old MacDonald Had a Farm." Each time you sing it, substitute a new animal. Allow the children to suggest animals for subsequent verses.

God made all the world we see.
Take a look around.
In this world, He made some cows.
This is how they sound:
With a "Moo, Moo," here,
And a "Moo, Moo," there,
Here a "Moo," there a "Moo,"
Everywhere a "Moo, Moo."
God made all the world we see.
Take a look around.

Suggestions:

horses—neigh, dogs—ruff, ducks—quack

Creation

continued

Creation March

Celebrate God's creation together with this stimulating march! Get a metronome, a small drum, or rhythm sticks someone can use to play a slow, steady beat. Before you begin the march, practice the motions below with the children.

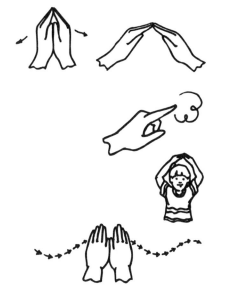

mountains: Peak fingertips together (pointing upward) in front of face and then lower hands to make the shape of a mountaintop.

clouds: Point up with both index fingers and make loops in the air.

sun: Lift arms above head to make a big circle. Allow only fingertips to touch just above head.

river: Put hands in front of you, palms down, and make a motion like the current of a river, with both hands moving side to side and up and down.

When you are ready to begin, stand together in a circle. Have someone slowly and rhythmically hit the drum. Teach the children to walk in a circle, taking one step for each drum beat. Practice this before you add in the movements (below).

When the children are ready, repeat the rhyme below, leading them in the motions, until they can say and do it with you.

1	2	3	4	
See the	mountains	God	made.	(*The circle walks right and does the "mountains" motions.*)
See the	sun up	in the	sky.	(*The circle walks right and does "sun" motions.*)
Hear the	river	waters	run.	(*The circle faces the center and does "river" motions.*)
Watch the	clouds as	they go	by.	(*The circle faces the center and does the "clouds" motions.*)
Thank You,	God.	Thank You,	God.	(*Everyone walks to the middle of the circle until shoulders are touching.*)
Thank You,	God, for	all the	earth.	(*Have the children put their arms on the shoulders of their neighbors.*)

Noah

(Genesis 6–9)

What a fun finger play for the children to do to remember this favorite story!

This Old Man, Noah

(Tune: "This Old Man")

This old man, he made one   (*Show left index finger.*)
Ark to save his wife and sons.   (*Cup hands like a boat.*)

Chorus:

For the 40 days the rain was   (*Wiggle fingers in a*
  falling down,   *downward motion.*)
God kept Noah safe and   (*Fold arms across*
  sound.   *chest for safety.*)

This old man, he made two   (*Show two fingers*
                           on right hand.)

Places for the animals God   (*Make those two*
  brought through.   *fingers "walk."*)

Repeat Chorus

This old man, he had three   (*Show three fingers*
                           on right hand.)

Sons to help him sail the sea.   (*Sway hands like*
                           waves.)

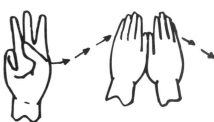 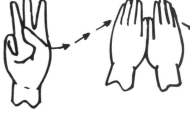

Repeat Chorus

This old man, he made four   (*Show four fingers*
                           on right hand.)

Locks to use to shut the door.   (*Clap hands*
                           together
                           on "shut.")

Repeat Chorus

This old man, he made five   (*Show five fingers*
                           on right hand.)

Bins of food to keep all alive.   (*Clap to the beat.*)

Noah

continued

Who Was in the Boat?

This finger play is a lot of fun for the children and will help them remember who all got in Noah's big boat.

Who was in the boat when the rain began to fall?
Noah and his wife, Noah and his wife   *(Show right and left fingers.)*

Who was in the boat when the rain began to fall?
Noah's three sons, Noah's three sons   *(Show three fingers on right hand.)*

Who was in the boat when the rain began to fall?
Noah's sons' wives, Noah's sons' wives   *(Show three fingers on left hand.)*

Who was in the boat when the rain began to fall?
All of the animals, two by two   *(Show both thumbs.)*

Who was in the boat when the rain began to fall?
Noah and his wife and his sons and their wives   *(Repeat motions for each.)*
And all of the animals, two by two

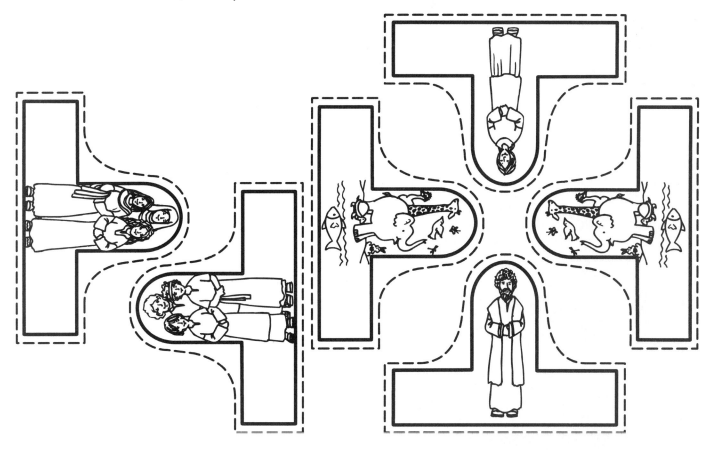

Noah

Noah March

This march is a fun way for children to remember who God wanted on Noah's ark. Gather in a circle, with everyone standing. Walk in place, creating a steady beat for this march-in-place rhythm. When you begin, repeat the first two lines until everyone is walking and speaking together (as much as is possible).

1	2	3	4
step	*step*	*step*	*step*

(Using the index and middle fingers of both hands, show your fingers walking.)

The animals	walked in,	two by	two—
The animals	walked in,	two by	two—

(Lean over and hang one arm down low, swinging it from side to side like a trunk.)

The elephants	with their	trunks down	low.
The elephants	with their	trunks down	low.

(With thumbs together, wave your fingers as if flapping wings.)

The animals	flew in,	two by	two—
The animals	flew in,	two by	two—

(First raise one hand with a wing flapping and then the other.)

The yellow ca-	nary and the	white dove,	too.
The yellow ca-	nary and the	white dove,	too.

(Lay one hand on top of the other and dip up and down slowly, like a worm crawling.)

The animals	crawled in,	two by	two.
The animals	crawled in,	two by	two.

(Continue same motion.)

The itty bitty	snail was a-	moving	slow.
The itty bitty	snail was a-	moving	slow.

(Hold hands in front of you like squirrel paws and make hopping motions.)

The animals	hopped in,	two by	two—
The animals	hopped in,	two by	two—

(Jump in place until you end.)

The green grass-	hopper and the	kanga-	roo.
The green grass-	hopper and the	kanga-	roo.

© Shining Star Publications

Abraham

(Genesis 12)

Abraham—A Special Man

Abraham was chosen by God to be the father of many nations. Help the children learn all about him by saying the words below as a rhyme. (Or, use the melody on page 12.) If you say them as a rhyme, you'll need a small drum or rhythm sticks and someone to play a slow, steady beat.

Begin by standing in a circle with everyone facing the center.

	Abraham traveled to a foreign land,	*(The circle walks to the right.)*
	Just because God told him to.	*(Everyone faces the center and walks in place.)*
	Abraham was a part of God's great plan,	*(The circle walks to the left.)*
	Just because he followed through.	*(Everyone faces the center and walks in place.)*
	Abraham was a man of faith.	*(Put right fist into left palm to show resolve.)*
	When God spoke, Abraham obeyed.	*(Shake finger as if telling someone something.)*
	I want to if I can, be like Abraham.	*(Point to self with right thumb.)*

Abraham

continued

Abraham

A-bra-ham —— trav-eled to a for-eign land—— Just be-cause—— God told him to.—

A-bra-ham—— was a part of God's great plan—— Just be-cause—— he fol-lowed through.—

A-bra-ham was a man of faith. When God spoke, A-bra-ham o-beyed. I want to if I can be like A - bra - ham.—

A-bra-ham—— trav-eled to a for-eign land.—— Just be-cause—— God told him to.—

A-bra-ham—— was a part of God's great plan—— Just be-cause—— he fol-lowed through.—

SS48843

Jacob and Joseph

(Genesis 37–46)

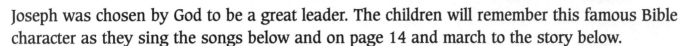

Joseph was chosen by God to be a great leader. The children will remember this famous Bible character as they sing the songs below and on page 14 and march to the story below.

A Man Named Jacob

(Tune: "Itsy Bitsy Spider")

There was a man named Jacob. God named him Israel.
He wanted sons, and so God gave him twelve.
They moved to Egypt because they had no food,
And they became a nation as the family grew and grew.

A Boy Named Joseph

Select a path you and the children can use to march around the room as you literally walk through the story. In essence, you will be recreating Joseph's travels to check on his brothers in the fields and then on to Egypt. First, gather in a circle. Read the first two verses (below). Then follow the leader around the room, singing the first refrain (see below and page 14, "Go Joseph . . ."). Gather again in a circle as you read verse 3, and then travel during the next refrain. Continue this way, reading verses 4 and 5 and singing the last refrain. Someone can play a soft, slow beat to march to in between verses.

1. Joseph was a little boy with a coat of many colors.
   God told Joseph in a dream he would be a leader one day.

2. Joseph's father sent Joseph to find his brothers in the field.
   Joseph took his coat and was on his way.

refrain: Go Joseph, find your brothers. (Repeat 4 times; see page 14.)

3. Joseph's brothers were not kind. They hurt Joseph when he found them.
   They sent Joseph away with strangers. The strangers took Joseph to Egypt.

refrain: Go Joseph, go to Egypt. (Repeat 4 times; see page 14.)

4. Joseph became a leader in Egypt. He learned to help the king.
   When Joseph's brother's needed food, they came to him to ask.

5. Joseph could have hurt his brothers. Joseph could have been so angry.
   But instead he just forgave them, and he finally got to see his father again.

refrain: Go Joseph, see your father. (Repeat 4 times; see page 14.)

Jacob and Joseph

continued

Go Joseph

Go Jo - seph, find your broth - ers. Go Jo - seph, find your broth - ers.

Go Jo - seph, find your broth - ers. Go Jo - seph, find your broth - ers.

Go Jo - seph, go to E - gypt. Go Jo - seph, go to E - gypt.

Go Jo - seph, go to E - gypt. Go Jo - seph, go to E - gypt.

Go Jo - seph, see your fath - er. Go Jo - seph, see your fath - er.

Go Jo - seph, see your fath - er. Go Jo - seph, see your fath - er.

 SS48843

Baby Moses

(Exodus 2:1–10)

Lullaby for Moses

Moses was special to God. God wanted him to lead His people out of Egypt. Teach the children all about Moses with the stories, songs, and activities below and on page 16.

Gather the children in a circle. Have them sit on their knees. You will need a basket with a cover. Tell the children the story of baby Moses below.

Moses' mother loved her baby son very much. She knew she had to hide him as it was a very dangerous time for little baby boys in Egypt. The pharaoh had said that all Israelite baby boys had to die. Moses' mother made a basket *(move hands as if weaving)* and coated it with tar so no water could get inside. Then she went with Miriam, Moses' big sister, down to the Nile River. There were reeds growing there that would hide the basket.

Moses' mother pushed the basket just a little way into the water and told Miriam to stay and watch it. *(Place basket in the middle of the circle.)*

Imagine Miriam's surprise when the princess came walking by. She saw the little basket and scooped up Moses. She said, "I'll adopt this baby as my own."

Miriam was a quick thinker. She ran up to the princess and said, "Would you like me to get a Hebrew woman to take care of him?" The princess said, "Yes." Guess who Miriam ran to get? Her own mother!

This is why Moses grew up safe and sound to lead God's people out of Egypt.

Now sing this lullaby to Moses with the children. (The melody is on page 16.)

Little baby in a basket,	*(Cup hands together.)*
Floating on the water,	*(Sway cupped hands back and forth.)*
When the princess found him there,	*(Point.)*
She became his mother.	
Chorus:	
Baby Moses,	*(Continue to cradle the "baby"*
God saved you,	*throughout the chorus.)*
So you could save your people,	
And lead them out of Egypt.	
God will tell you what to do.	

SS48843

Baby Moses

continued

Baby Moses

Lit - tle ba - by in a bas - ket, Float - ing on the wa - ter,

When the prin - cess found him there, She be - came his moth - er.

Ba - by Mo - ses, God saved you, So

you could save your peo - ple, And lead them out of E - gypt.

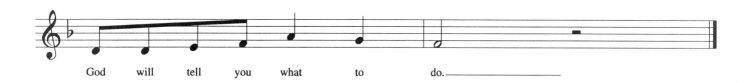

God will tell you what to do. _____

16

SS48843

Moses as a Man

(Exodus 3)

God saved Moses for a special reason—to save His people! The children can learn all about this as they say this rhyme and do the motions (or use the melody on page 18). If you choose to say it, have the children sit with you in a circle. Teach the children to make this rhythm by clapping their hands on their knees two times and then together once.

The Burning Bush

1	2	3	4
(clap knees)	(clap knees)	(clap hands)	(nothing)

Once the children can keep the rhythm going, teach them this rhyme.

1	2	3	4
God		came	to
Mo-	ses	in	a
bur-		ning	
bush,			a
bush		that	
ne-	ver	burned	
down.			
X	X	X	X
God		came	to
Mo-	ses	in	a
bur-		ning	
bush,			and
He		sent	
Mo-	ses	to	
town			
to		say:	
"Phar-		aoh,	
Phar-		aoh,	
let	my	peo-	ple
go.			
Phar-		aoh,	
Phar-		aoh,	
let	my	peo-	ple
go!"			

1

2

3

4

SS48843

Moses as a Man

continued

Let My People Go

God came to Mo-ses in a burn-ing bush, a

bush that ne-ver burned down.

God came to Mo-ses in a burn-ing bush, and

He sent Mo-ses to town to say:

Phar-aoh, Phar-aoh, let my peo-ple go,

Phar-aoh, Phar-aoh, let my peo-ple go!

SS48843

The Exodus

(Exodus 3)

The Manna Song

Moses led God's people out of Egypt to the Promised Land. They were called Hebrews and Israelites. These people traveled through the wilderness for many years. Share this story with the children and then sing the song below.

The Exodus

continued

The Manna Song continued

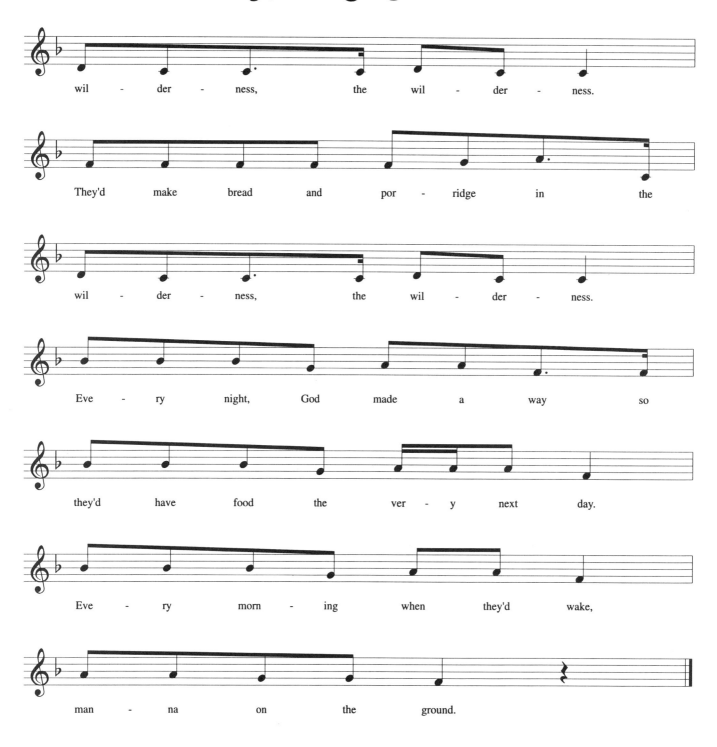

wil - der - ness, the wil - der - ness.

They'd make bread and por - ridge in the

wil - der - ness, the wil - der - ness.

Eve - ry night, God made a way so

they'd have food the ver - y next day.

Eve - ry morn - ing when they'd wake,

man - na on the ground.

SS48843

The Judges

(Judges 4–5, 6–8, 13 and 16)

God chose some very special leaders to guide His people. They were called judges. Read about these leaders to or with the children. Then teach them the song below.

After Josh-ua ruled the He-brews, And be-fore they crowned King Saul, Is - ra - el was ruled by judg - es,

Fine Verse 1

Who helped peo-ple keep the law. Debo-rah sat be-neath a palm tree, Help - ing peo - ple choose what's right.

Verse 2

She be-came a sol-dier. God helped her win the fight. Gid-e-on be-came a sol-dier, E - ven though he was a - fraid.

Verse 3

Yet he won a bat-tle, God an-swered when he prayed. Sam - son was the strong - est man, That

Repeat Chorus
D. C. al Fine

an - y-one had ev - er seen. He made fool-ish choic-es And final - ly lost his strength.

SS48843

David

(1 Samuel 17)

David and Goliath

Children love the story of David and Goliath. They will love acting it out using copies of the finger puppets below and on page 23 and singing about it, too (page 23)!

Puppets:

young David (right thumb)
Goliath (left index finger)
King Saul (right index finger)
Saul's army (right middle finger)

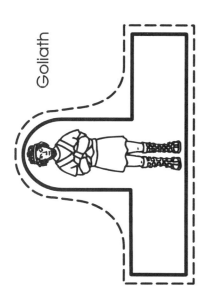

Goliath

David was a young man who loved God and played the harp. (*Hold up the David puppet.*) His job was to take care of his father's sheep.

King Saul (*hold up the King Saul puppet*) was the king of Israel. He was very unhappy sometimes. He asked David to come and play his harp. This made Saul feel better.

So David spent some of his time with King Saul (*show both puppets*) and some of his time at home taking care of the sheep (*show only David*).

Once while David was with King Saul and his army (*show all three puppets*), a big, bad man named Goliath attacked them. (*Show Goliath puppet.*) He said, "Hey, you people from Israel. Let's see if you can beat me. I don't think you can. Will your God help you?"

The army was scared of Goliath. When David saw this, he couldn't believe it. He said, "We have God on our side. How can you be scared of this giant?"

David collected some rocks for his slingshot and went out to face Goliath. (*Move David and Goliath puppets closer together.*)

David took a stone out of his pouch and started swinging it around and around and around. (*Swing the David puppet around as you speak.*) Then POP! He shot the rock and hit Goliath in the head. (*Have the Goliath puppet fall down.*)

David won the battle! Even though he was young and had only a slingshot, he won because he believed God could help him win. Everyone cheered (*move right hand puppets up and down*) except the other army.

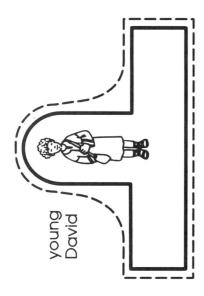

young David

SS48843

David

continued

Use your puppets to celebrate as you sing the song below.

David Won the Battle

Da - vid won the bat - tle. He
made the gi - ants leave.
Da - vid won the bat - tle, Be -
cause he be - lieved.

David and Goliath Puppet Patterns

King Saul

Saul's army

SS48843

Daniel

(Daniel 6)

The story of Daniel is a favorite of many children. Teach the children the song and motions below and then teach them about Shadrach, Meshach, and Abednego with the song on page 25.

Daniel's Praying

(Tune: "Frère Jacques")

Daniel's praying,
 Daniel's praying,

(Place hands in front, palms together, as if praying.)

In his home,
 in his home.

Even though
 the king

Had told the
 people not to,

(Shake finger in front as if confronting someone.)

Daniel prayed,
 Daniel prayed.

(Place hands in front, palms together, as if praying.)

Daniel's sleeping,
 Daniel's sleeping,

(Put hands together but to the side of face, as a pillow.)

With the lions, with
 the lions.

God will keep him
 safe, though.

(Point up, as if to God in heaven.)

God will keep him
 safe, though.

Daniel obeyed,
 Daniel obeyed.

(Clap to the rhythm.)

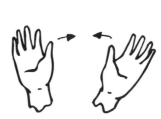

Daniel

continued

They Would Not Bow Down

(Daniel 3)

Shad - rach, Mesh - ach, and - A - bed - ne - go, Would not wor-ship an - y - one but God.

E - ven though the king had told them so, They would not bow down. The

king had made a new rule: When you hear the trum - pet sound,

This is what you all must do, You bow down._____

Verse 2

When the trumpet sounded,
Everyone bowed to their knees.
Shadrach, Meshach, Abednego,
Stood to their feet.

Verse 3

So the king, he punished them,
Sent them to a fiery blaze.
But God watched them in the fire
And He kept them safe.

SS48843

Elijah

(1 Kings 18:16–39)

Elijah was one of God's great prophets. The children can learn all about him as they say the rhyme below or sing it as a song on page 27.

Have the children sit in a circle on their knees. Tell the children to imagine that there are logs on each side of them. They should imagine that the space in the middle of the circle is where Elijah was to build his altar. As you say this rhyme, have each child reach first to the right and pick up a brick and put it in front of him or her to help build the altar. Then each child reaches to the left and makes the same motion. (Suggestion: If you have enough blocks in your room, you might want to actually build an altar during the first part of this rhyme.)

	X		X		X		X	
E-	li-	jah	built	an	al-	tar		to
	(Pick up to the right.)		*(Place on altar.)*		*(Pick up to the left.)*	*(Place on altar.)*		
	show	the	one	true	God.			He
	(Pick up to the right.)		*(Place on altar.)*		*(Pick up to the left.)*	*(Place on altar.)*		
	built	it	on	Mt.	Car-	mel,		
	(Pick up to the right.)		*(Place on altar.)*		*(Pick up to the left.)*	*(Place on altar.)*		
	way	up	at	the	top.			E-
	(Pick up to the right.)		*(Place on altar.)*		*(Pick up to the left.)*	*(Place on altar.)*		
	li-	jah	prayed	to	God			to
	(Sit back on knees with hands folded in prayer.)							
	send	a	fire	down,			to	
	(Still sitting back on knees, open hands up about two feet and look up at the ceiling.)							
	burn	up	all	the	al-	tar		and
	(Stand during this line and the next.)							
	prove	He	was	a-	round.			

Say the rest of this:

And then fire fe-l-l-l-l-l-l-l from heaven . . .

(On the word "fell," stand on tiptoes, stretch arms up, and wiggle fingers as you lower arms to show the fire falling.)

. . . and showed everyone there that God was the ONE TRUE God. *(Emphasize "ONE TRUE God" by holding up index finger and shaking on each word.)*

     SS48843

Elijah

continued

Elijah Built an Altar

E - li - jah built an al - tar to

show there is a God. He built it on Mt. Car - mel,

way up at the top. E - li - jah prayed to God to

send a fi - re down, To burn up all the al - tar and

prove He was a - round.

SS48843

Good Queen Esther

(Esther)

Good Queen Esther

Esther was special to the Jewish people because she saved them all from harm and a mean man named Haman. Share this story with the children. Use the patterns on page 29 to make finger puppets for the children to use as you walk through the story of good Queen Esther.

Puppets:
Esther (right index finger)
the other girls (right middle finger)
the king (left index finger)
the people (left middle finger)
Haman (left thumb)

The king was looking for a wife. (*Hold up king puppet; move him around in his search.*) The king was looking for a queen.

Many young girls came to say that they would be his queen. (*Hold up girls and Esther puppets on right hand.*)

The king was looking for a woman just as special as could be. (*Have the king look over the girls and Esther puppets.*) When he saw Esther, he knew that she would be his queen. (*Lower the girls puppet, leaving only Esther and king.*)

Queen Esther saw an evil man (*show Queen Esther and Haman*) who planned to kill her people. So she told her husband-king about what this man would do. (*Move Esther as if she's talking to the king.*)

Because Queen Esther was so brave (*hold up only Esther*), she saved her very own people (*hold up Esther and the people on your left hand*), so they could worship God until they traveled back to their homeland.

Good Queen Esther

continued

Good Queen Esther Puppet Patterns (for page 28)

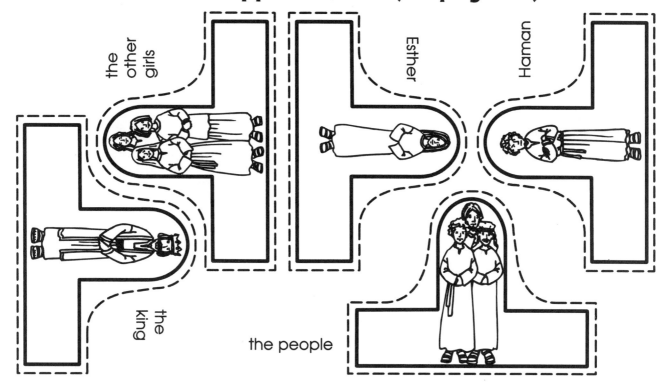

the other girls

Esther

Haman

the king

the people

Ruth Finds a New Home Puppet Patterns (for page 30)

Obed

Naomi

Boaz

Ruth

SS48843

Ruth

(Ruth)

Ruth Finds a New Home

What a wonderful story to tell using finger puppets! Ruth is a wonderful example of loyalty and love for children—and everyone! Have each child make the finger puppets on page 29 and follow your actions as you tell the story.

Puppets:
Ruth (right index finger)
Naomi (left index finger)
Boaz (right middle finger)
Obed (right ring finger)

Naomi wanted to travel back home. (*Hold up Naomi puppet.*) She told her daughter-in-law, Ruth, that she was leaving. (*Have the two puppets "talk" to each other.*) Ruth said, "Oh, no, Naomi. I have come to love you too much. I'll go with you wherever you go." (*Have the two puppets "hug."*)

Ruth and Naomi traveled together (*hold up puppets on both index fingers*) from Moab to Bethlehem. (*Move puppets from one side of your body to the other as if walking.*) In their new home, Ruth met a man named Boaz. She gathered grain in his fields. (*Raise the Boaz puppet.*) He became her husband. (*Move fingers together.*)

Ruth and Boaz had a baby. (*Raise the ring finger with the baby puppet.*) They named him Obed. They were a family. Naomi was his grandmother. (*Move the Naomi puppet close to the family.*) She helped take care of him. Because Ruth loved Naomi and was a loyal friend, (*hold up Naomi and Ruth puppets*) she found her own family—a husband and a baby. (*Hold up all puppets.*) Sometimes good things happen to us because we do the right thing for other people.

SS48843

Psalms

(Psalms)

The book of Psalms is filled with wonderful information we can use to help us grow in our love of God. Sing the songs below and on page 32 with the children. Discuss the Bible verses with them and their importance in the children's lives.

Come, let us bow down in worship, let us kneel before the Lord our Maker; for he is our God and we are the people of his pasture, the flock under his care. (Psalm 95:6–7)

When We Worship God

When we wor-ship God, we tell Him how great we know He is.

When we wor-ship God, we tell Him how glad we are that

He is our God, And He is our king, And

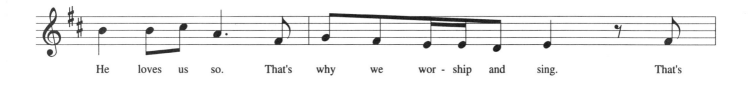

He loves us so. That's why we wor-ship and sing. That's

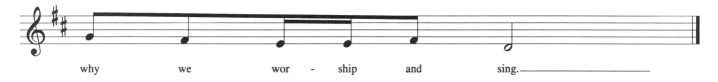

why we wor-ship and sing.

Psalms

continued

Worship the Lord with gladness; come before him with joyful songs. Know that the Lord is God. It is he who made us, and we are his; we are his people, the sheep of his pasture. (Psalm 100:2–3)

One True God

Lord, we know You're the one true God. We are glad to wor-ship You.

Lord, we know that You made the world And You made us, too.

Lord, we know that You'll al - ways be Right be - side us all the way.

Lord, we know You're the one true God. We wor - ship You to - day.

The New Testament

SS48843

Jesus' Birth

(Luke 1:26–38; 2:8–20; Matthew 1:18–25)

Jesus' birth was such a blessed event for all Christians. Help the children learn all about it as they clap out the story below or sing the song on page 35.

An Angel Came

Have the children sit in a circle with their legs crossed. Teach the children the rhythm below. They clap their hands on their knees and then clap their hands together.

1	2	3	4
(clap right knee)	(clap left knee)	(clap hands)	(clap hands)

Once the children can keep the rhythm going, teach them this rhyme:

1	2	3	4
The angel	came to	Mary and	said,
"You're going to	have a	ba-	by.
You'll be glad He	came.	Jesus is His	name.
He's going to	be a	king."	
The angel	came to	Joseph and	said,
"Mary's going to	have a	ba-	by.
You'll be glad He	came.	Jesus is His	name.
He's going to	be a	king."	
The angel	came to the	shepherds and	said,
"Somebody's	had a	ba-	by.
You'll be glad He	came.	Jesus is His	name.
He's going to	be a	king."	

SS48843

Jesus' Birth

continued

The Angel Came

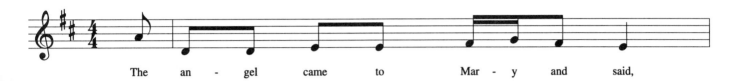

The an - gel came to Mar - y and said,

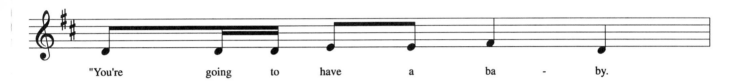

"You're going to have a ba - by.

You'll be glad He came. Je - sus is His name.

He's going to be a king."

Verse 2

The angel came to Joseph and said,

"Mary's going to have a baby.

You'll be glad He came. Jesus is His name.

He's going to be a king."

Verse 3

The angel came to the shepherds and said,

"Somebody's had a baby.

You'll be glad He came. Jesus is His name.

He's going to be a king."

SS48843

Jesus' Healings

The children can better understand Jesus' great power when they learn how He healed many sick people. Teach them the finger plays below and on page 37. Make copies of all the puppet patterns for you (and the children if you want) to use to dramatize the story below.

The Hem of His Garment (Luke 8:43–48)

Use the finger puppets on page 37 and this script to tell the story of a brave woman and the power of Jesus.

Puppets:

Jesus (right index finger), lady (left index finger), two small crowd scenes (right and left middle fingers)

Jesus was walking through a crowd of people. (*Hold up both hands with puppets showing. Bob as if walking.*)

In that crowd, there was a woman who had a blood disease. She snuck up behind Jesus and touched the edge of His coat hoping that His great power would heal her. All at once, she was well! (*Move left index finger to signify the woman. Use your left hand to let her sneak up behind Jesus and touch His clothes.*)

"Who touched me?" Jesus asked. (*Stop hands from moving. Move right index finger to signify Jesus talking.*)

No one answered. The woman stood back in the crowd. She didn't know if she had done something wrong. (*Move left index finger close to left crowd as if the woman is hiding in the crowd.*)

Jesus' disciples said, "Jesus, there are many people here. What do you mean, 'Who touched me?'" (*Move right crowd as if the disciples are talking from the crowd.*)

But Jesus said, "I know someone touched me, and my power went out to them." (*Move right index finger to signify Jesus talking.*)

Finally, the lady knew she would have to admit it. She was trembling and nervous, but she bowed at Jesus' feet and told Him that she had been healed when she touched Him. (*Separate fingers of left hand to show the lady walking to Jesus. Lower finger for her to bow.*)

Jesus wasn't angry. He was glad. He said, "Your faith in me healed you. Congratulations!" (*Have Jesus face the lady as He speaks to her.*)

Jesus' Healings

Ten Men Finger Play (Luke 17:11–19)

Ten men with leprosy—   (*Hold up 10 fingers.*)

All were healed by Jesus.

But only one   (*Hold up only one thumb.*)

Ever came to say "Thank You."

"Where were the other nine?"   (*Hold up all fingers except that one thumb.*)

Jesus asked, Jesus asked.

But only one, only one   (*Hold up only one thumb.*)

Ever came to say "Thank You."

The Hem of His Garment Puppet Patterns

Jesus

lady

crowd

crowd

     37   SS48843

Jesus' Miracles

Jesus performed many incredible miracles. The children can learn some of them by doing the finger play below and by singing the songs below and on page 39.

Healing a Blind Man (John 9:1–7)

Jesus saw a blind man

(*Place a hand over each eye like a patch.*)

Who wished that he could see.

(*Open fingers on hands and peek out from between them.*)

Jesus made some mud.

(*Kneel down and rub the floor with two fingers.*)

Then He smoothed the mud on the man's eyes.

(*Using the index and middle fingers of both hands, lightly rub in front of your eyes, but don't actually rub eyes.*)

Jesus sent the man to a pool to wash off the mud.

(*Scoop hands to face as if there is water in them.*)

When the man did, he could see!

(*Put hands over face on last "scoop of water" and then open hands with a smile.*)

Close the story of the healing of the blind man by singing the song below.

(Tune: "The Farmer in the Dell")

The blind man now could see.
The blind man now could see.
Jesus worked a miracle.
The blind man now could see.

Miracles

Je - sus could turn water into wine. He could make a lame man walk.

He could heal the blind. He could work a mir - a - cle an - y place or time.

Je - sus could turn wa - ter in - to wine. Je - sus could raise a

per - son from the dead. He could feed a crowd with on - ly fish and bread.

He could make a storm stop, just be - cause He said. He could raise a per - son from the

dead. Je - sus could do mir - a - cles.

He was the Son of God. Je - sus could do

mir - a - cles. He was the Son of God.

SS48843

Jesus' Parables

Jesus told stories, or parables, to help people learn about God and His Word. Help the children better understand some of the parables by discussing the Bible verses and related stories listed below and on page 41. Then teach them the songs.

He replied, "Because you have so little faith. I tell you the truth, if you have faith as small as a mustard seed, you can say to this mountain, 'Move from here to there' and it will move. Nothing will be impossible for you." (Matthew 17:20)

"It is like a mustard seed, which is the smallest seed you plant in the ground. Yet when planted, it grows and becomes the largest of all garden plants, with such big branches that the birds of the air can perch in its shade." (Mark 4:31–32)

Have Faith in God

SS48843

Jesus' Parables

continued

"Suppose one of you has a hundred sheep and loses one of them. Does he not leave the ninety-nine in the open country and go after the lost sheep until he finds it? And when he finds it, he joyfully puts it on his shoulders and goes home. Then he calls his friends and neighbors together and says, 'Rejoice with me; I have found my lost sheep.' I tell you that in the same way there will be more rejoicing in heaven over one sinner who repents than over ninety-nine righteous persons who do not need to repent." (Luke 15:4–7)

A Shepherd

How much does a shepherd love his lamb? How far will he go to find it? How much does a shepherd love his lamb? So much that he would go over the mountain and through the dark, to find the lamb that he had lost, over the mountain and through the dark, to find his little lamb.

Verse 2:

How much does our Father love His child?
How far will He go to help Him?
How much does our Father love His child?
So much that He would go

Wherever He needed, no matter the cost,
To help the child who felt so lost.
Wherever He needed, no matter the cost,
To help His little child.

SS48843

Jesus Is . . .

(John 14:6; Isaiah 9:6; John 10:14)

Jesus is so many wonderful things. Teach the children about some of these things with the chant and finger play below. Or, have them sing it using the song on page 43.

Have the children sit in a circle cross-legged. Teach the children the simple rhythm below.

1	2	3	4
(touch the floor)	(clap on legs)	(clap hands)	(clap hands)

Once the children are familiar with the rhythm, say the rhyme, letting them repeat each line.

	1	2	3	4
The	Bible	says	(The Bible	says)
	Jesus	is	(Jesus	is)
The	Prince of	Peace.	(The Prince of	Peace.)
	Jesus	is	(Jesus	is)
	The Good	Shepherd.	(The Good	Shepherd.)
	Jesus	is . . .	(Jesus	is . . .)
	He is the	way.	(He is the	way.)
	He is the	truth.	(He is the	truth.)
	He is the	life.	(He is the	life.)
	Jesus	is . . .	(Jesus	is . . .)

Only One Way

Jesus answered, "I am the way and the truth and the life. No one comes to the Father except through me." (John 14:6)

Teacher: How many ways to the Father? *(Put hands out to the side, shoulder high, palms up.)*

Children: Only one way—Jesus. *(Hold up index finger.)*

Teacher: How many ways to the Father? *(Put hands out to the side, shoulder high, palms up.)*

Children: Only one way—Jesus. *(Hold up index finger.)*

Teacher: Not two ways? *(Hold up two fingers.)*

Children: Just one way. *(Hold up index finger.)*

Teacher: Not three ways? *(Hold up three fingers.)*

Children: Just one way. *(Hold up index finger.)*

Teacher: How many ways to the Father? *(Put hands out to the side, shoulder high, palms up.)*

Children: Only one way—Jesus. *(Hold up index finger.)*

Once your children know this well, have some fun with it by asking many different numbers (example: not 1000 ways?).

Jesus Is . . .

Jesus Is . . .

The Bi - ble says (The Bi - ble says)_____ Je - sus

is (Je - sus is) The Prince of Peace (The Prince of

Peace)_____ Je - sus is_____ (Je - sus is) The Good Shep -

herd (The Good Shep - herd)_____ Je - sus is (Je - sus

is)_____ He is the way_____ (He is the way)_____ He is the

truth_____ (He is the truth)_____ He is the life_____ (He is the

life)_____ Je - sus is (Je - sus is)_____

Jesus' Friends

Jesus had so many wonderful, helpful, and interesting friends. Teach the children about some of them by completing the activities below and on pages 45–46.

Nicodemus (John 3:1–21)

Read the story of Nicodemus to the children. Talk about how important faith and believing in God is before you sing this song.

Ni - co - de - mus said to Je - sus, "You are more than just a man."

Ni - co - de - mus said to Je - sus, "How can I be born a - gain?"

Je - sus said, "God loves this world and wants us all to live for - ev - er!

So He sent His one and on - ly Son to set us free.

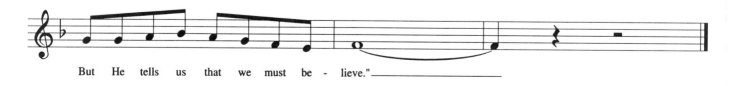

But He tells us that we must be - lieve."

SS48843

Jesus' Friends

Zacchaeus (Luke 19:1–10)

Read this story to the children. Discuss with the children how Jesus befriended even sinners—happily. Then teach them the song and motions below.

Zacch - ae - us climbed a tree Be - cause he want-ed to see Je - sus walk - ing by in

Jer - i - cho one day. And just when Je - sus passed, He looked up and He asked, "Zacch -

ae - us, may I vis - it you to - day?" Zacch - ae - us learned a bet - ter way. When

he spent time with Je - sus that day, he be - gan to do as he should. Je - sus helped him know he could.

Once the children have learned this song, add these motions. Begin by gathering the children in a circle, facing to the right.

Zacchaeus climbed a tree	*(Circle to the right, making climbing motions with hands.)*
Because he wanted to see	*(Face middle with one hand over eyes as if looking.)*
Jesus walking by in Jericho one day.	*(Point downward as if to see Jesus passing.)*
And just when Jesus passed,	*(Hold hands with the people on both sides and circle left.)*
He looked up and He asked,	*(Continue to circle.)*
"Zacchaeus, may I visit you today?"	*(Stop, face middle, and swing arms, still holding hands.)*

(Clap lightly during the chorus.)

45 SS48843

Jesus' Friends

continued

Mary and Martha (Luke 10:38–42)

Mary and Martha were special friends of Jesus. Mary loved to sit and listen to Him talk. The children can learn all about these two very different sisters by using the finger puppets below to tell this story.

Puppets:

Mary (left thumb), Martha (right index finger), Jesus (left index finger)

Mary and Martha were sisters. (*Hold up Mary and Martha puppets.*) They were very different. (*Have puppets face each other.*)

Martha was a busy person around the house. (*Make Martha puppet zip around fast, here and there, back and forth.*)

Mary liked to sit back and enjoy people and things. (*Hold Mary still and make a big, contented sigh.*)

One day, Jesus came to visit. (*Show index finger puppet of Jesus and walk Him into the scene.*) Martha was so excited. She hurried around getting ready. (*Martha puppet zips around more.*)

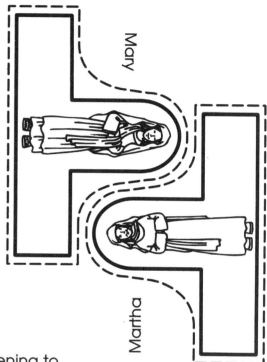

Mary wasn't rushing around. She was just sitting and listening to Jesus talk. (*Move thumb and index finger as if they are interacting.*)

When Martha saw that Mary wasn't helping, she went to Jesus and complained. "Jesus, make Mary help me!" Martha said to Jesus. (*Indicate Martha talking to Jesus.*)

Jesus said, "Martha, please understand, you'll always have some cleaning and cooking to do, but I won't always be here. Mary is doing the right thing." (*Indicate Jesus talking to Martha.*)

We all need to remember how smart Mary was. We need to take time to listen to Jesus, too. (*Hold up Jesus puppet.*)

Close the story with this song.

(Tune: "Itsy Bitsy Spider")

Mary and Martha lived in a small town.
Jesus came to visit them when ever He came 'round.
Martha rushed around to keep the house in order,
But Mary sat with Jesus and just listened to Him speak.

SS48843

Jesus' Death and Resurrection

(Matthew 27–28)

What a sad event Jesus' death was—but how miraculous was His resurrection! Let the children sing the song below and the one on page 48 to learn all about these two events.

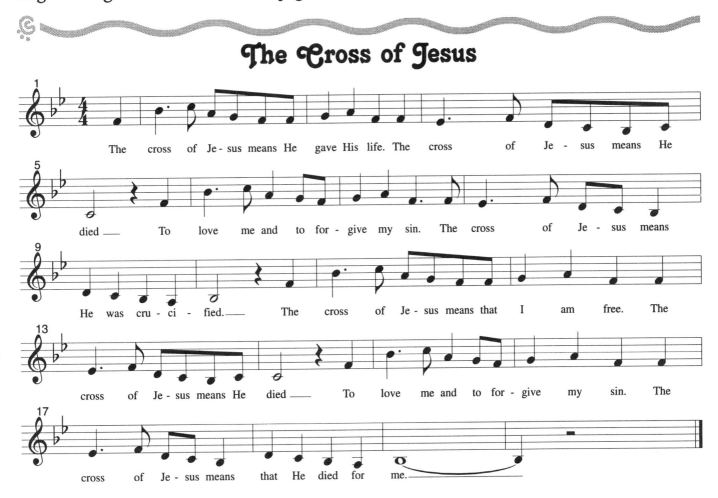

After you learn this song, you may want to try these motions with it.

The cross of Jesus means He gave His life. *(Use right hand to draw a cross in the air in front of you.)*
The cross of Jesus means He died *(Use right hand to draw a cross in the air in front of you.)*
To love me and to forgive my sin. *(Point to yourself, then cover your heart with the same hand.)*
The cross of Jesus means He was crucified. *(Cross arms over chest, palms open.)*

The cross of Jesus means that I am free. *(Use right hand to draw a cross in the air in front of you.)*
The cross of Jesus means He died *(Use right hand to draw a cross in the air in front of you.)*
To love me and to forgive my sin. *(Point to yourself, then cover your heart with the same hand.)*
The cross of Jesus means that He died for me. *(Cross arms over chest, palms open.)*

Jesus' Death and Resurrection

continued

Jesus Is Alive (Matthew 28:1–10)

Mar - y was sad that her Lord had died. Je - sus was His name.

Mar - y had seen Him be cru - ci - fied. Je - sus was His name.

Ear - ly one morn - ing, she went to His grave. There she found a great sur - prise.

Chorus

Je - sus was gone! He was a - live! Je - sus is a - live!

Eve - ry - one can sing! Je - sus is a - live! He's our Lord and King.

SS48843

New Testament Missionaries

(Acts 6:1–7)

Gather the children in a circle. Use the script below and on page 50 to teach the children about the missionaries of the early church. Each time you come to the chorus, sing together and march to the right, as if you are traveling like those missionaries.

Practice the chorus a few times while you are marching so the children will be ready to participate.

Go Tell the World

Chorus:

1. After Jesus died, and then was raised back to life, and then went back to heaven, the disciples knew they had to let people know all about Jesus. That is when the church started. They began to meet to remember Jesus and to talk about serving Him. They began to send out missionaries.

Chorus

2. Paul was one of the first missionaries. He traveled to places like Corinth *(have the children repeat that name)* and Cyprus *(children repeat)* and Macedonia *(children repeat)*.

Chorus

3. Paul wasn't the only missionary. There was also Barnabas *(children repeat)*, Silas *(children repeat)*, and a young man named Timothy *(children repeat)*.

Chorus

New Testament Missionaries

continued

4. In many of the places Paul and the other missionaries went, churches were started. After the missionaries left, they wrote letters to those churches. Some of those letters became part of our Bible, like the books of Colossians *(children repeat)*, Ephesians *(children repeat)*, and Galatians *(children repeat)*.

Chorus

5. Today, we are all missionaries. We tell the people that we meet about Jesus' life and death and life again. We are all missionaries *(children repeat)*.

Chorus

Being a missionary . . .
   means telling someone "Jesus loves you."

Being a missionary . . .
   means loving others in all you do.

Being a missionary . . .
   means telling how Jesus came,
   to forgive our sins
   so we can begin
   to be missionaries.

Chorus

Go Tell the World

(Tune: "Three Blind Mice")

Go tell the world.
Go tell the world:
Jesus lives, Jesus lives.
He loves us happy and loves us sad.
He loves us laughing and loves us mad.
He loves us whether we're good or bad.
Go tell the world.
Go tell the world.

SS48843

The Good Samaritan

(Luke 10:25–37)

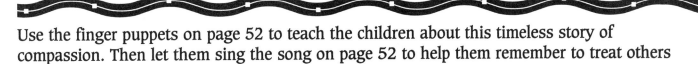

Use the finger puppets on page 52 to teach the children about this timeless story of compassion. Then let them sing the song on page 52 to help them remember to treat others kindly.

Puppets:

priest (left thumb)

Levite (left index finger)

Samaritan (right index finger)

hurt man (right thumb)

Someone in a crowd of people asked Jesus what a good neighbor is. Jesus answered them by telling this story:

A man was walking from Jerusalem to Jericho when he was attacked and hurt by robbers. (*Show hurt man puppet.*) They left him laying on the road.

A priest, a holy man, was walking by (*show priest bobbing by*) and saw the hurt man. But he didn't help him. In fact, he walked by on the other side of the road.

Then a Levite (*show Levite bobbing by*), someone who helps in the church, walked by and saw the hurt man. He didn't help him, either. He walked by on the other side of the road.

Finally, a Samaritan walked by. (*Show Samaritan.*) Some people thought Samaritans were not good people. But when he saw the hurt man, the Samaritan felt so sorry for him. The Samaritan put bandages on the man's hurt places and then gave him a ride on his donkey to an inn where they would take care of the man. The Samaritan even paid the bill for the poor, hurt man.

Now, the first two men were supposed to be really good men because they worked at church and helped out with good things. But according to this story, which man was the good neighbor to the hurt man? (*Hold up the three puppets and let the children answer by indicating a puppet.*)

Jesus told the people to be the kind of neighbor the Samaritan was. (*Show the Samaritan puppet.*) That's the kind of neighbor we should be.

SS48843

The Good Samaritan

continued

Sing this song together to close the story of "The Good Samaritan."

Be a Good Neighbor

Be a good neigh-bor when you can, When you can, give a help-ing hand,

Be a good neigh-bor when you can, just like Je - sus says.

The Good Samaritan Puppet Patterns

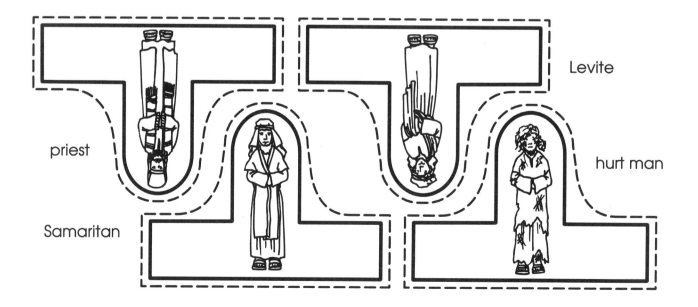

priest

Samaritan

Levite

hurt man

The Prodigal Son

(Luke 15:11–32)

father

younger son

pigs

older son

The Parable of the Lost Son

The children can learn about God's love for us as they use the finger puppets above to re-enact this story. Then let them sing the accompanying song on page 54.

Puppets:

the father (left index finger), the older son (left middle finger), the younger son (right index finger), pigs (right middle finger)

Jesus told this story about a man and his two sons:

There was a man who had two sons. (*Show all puppets except pigs.*)

The younger son (*show puppet*) said to his father (*show puppet*), "Father, give me my share of the money. I want to see the world." The father gave him his money and off he went. (*Younger son puppet skips off.*)

At first while he was traveling, the younger son had a great time buying things and having parties. He wasted his money until he had no money left. (*As you talk, move the little puppet slower and slower.*)

He finally got a horrible job feeding pigs. (*Show the pigs.*) He was so broke and so hungry that he even wished he could have the pigs' food.

One day, he thought, "You know what? My father's farm hands have it better than me. I'm going to go back to Dad and ask him if he'll hire me. I've been so bad that he probably won't even want to see me. But I'll try." (*The puppet starts toward home.*)

All the way home, the son practiced his speech. He got to where he could just barely see the house, and he saw someone running to meet him. (*Stretch your left arm far away and start the father puppet toward the son.*) Who could that be?

The Prodigal Son

continued

It was his father! The son started saying the speech he had practiced, but his dad wasn't even listening. He was hugging and kissing his son. He was taking him to the house. (*Start moving the puppets together.*) The father wasn't angry! He was thrilled to see his son. He was glad his son was home!

That evening, the father threw a big party for his son—a "Welcome Home" party. (Have *father and son puppets dancing around.*)

While they were celebrating, the older son came home from working. (*Show the older son.*) He was a little mad. He said, "Dad why are you giving him a party when I've been the faithful one? He's the one who ran away."

The father said, "Son, I know it's hard to understand, but whenever someone we love has been lost and then comes home, we just have to celebrate!" (*Have all three puppets dance around.*)

Think about how happy that dad was. (*Show father puppet.*) That's how God feels when we believe in Him. He feels like we just came home after being gone a long time. He is always happy to see us, no matter what we've done.

Use this song to summarize the story.

General Christian Concepts

SS48843

Obedience

The children can learn about the importance of obeying God's commandments as they sing this song and the one on page 57. Discuss the Bible verses with them and ways they can obey God's Word.

He replied, "Blessed rather are those who hear the word of God and obey it." (Luke 11:28)
Do not merely listen to the word, and so deceive yourselves. Do what it says. (James 1:22)

Blessed Are They

Bles - sed are they who hear God's Word, and o - bey and o - bey.

Bles - sed are they who hear God's Word, and o - bey what it says.

Bles - sed are they who are do - ers of the Word, and o - bey and o - bey.

Bles - sed are they who are do - ers of the Word, and o - bey what it says.

Obedience

continued

What Does It Mean?

This is the love for God: to obey his commands. And his commands are not burdensome.
(1 John 5:3)

What does it mean to love the Lord? To o - bey His com - mands.

What does it mean to love the Lord? To o - bey His com- mands.

What does it mean to o-bey the Lord? To do what He says in His Word.

What does it mean to o-bey the Lord? To do what He says in His Word.

The Church

(Acts)

The songs below and the one on page 59 are fun for the children to sing to learn all about church. Help them understand that church is much more than just a building.

Get Ready for Church

During this first verse, have the children stand in a circle, holding hands and circling to the right. On the other verses, act out the verse.

(Tune: "Mulberry Bush")

What do we do to get ready for church,
Ready for church, ready for church?
What do we do to get ready for church
To worship God with others?

(Take suggestions from the children and use them for other verses, such as "put on socks.")

(We put on our socks) to get ready for church,
Ready for church, ready for church.
(We put on our socks) to get ready for church
To worship God with others.

(Other suggestions: put on our shoes, put on our clothes, ride in the car, have a meal, park the car . . .)

Here in Church

This kind of familiar tune and simple words are good to sing as you are gathering together or even when you're picking up the room.

(Tune: "London Bridge")

Church is somewhere we can learn,
We can learn, we can learn.
Church is somewhere we can learn.
We can learn here.

Church is somewhere we are safe,
We are safe, we are safe.
Church is somewhere we are safe.
We are safe here.

Church is somewhere we can sing,
We can sing, we can sing.
Church is somewhere we can sing.
We can sing here.

Church is somewhere we are loved,
We are loved, we are loved.
Church is somewhere we are loved.
We are loved here.

The Church

My Church

My church is not the walls or the sign at the street. My church is the peo - ple in - side.—— My church is not the build - ings, it's the peo - ple I meet. My church is the peo - ple in - side.——— In - side these walls, we pray and love. In - side these walls, we give.——— In - side these walls, we wor - ship God a - bove, and learn to - geth - er how to live.———

SS48843

Joy

Joy is something everyone strives to have, and the rhyme below can help the children learn how to help others experience it.

A Smile

A cheerful look brings joy to the heart, and good news gives health to the bones.
(Proverbs 15:30)

Recite the rhyme below together using the finger puppets for emphasis. Put the smiling puppet on one index finger and the frowning puppet on the other index finger. (If possible, make a copy of the puppets for each child.) Hold up each puppet on the appropriate line. Bob it up and down on each of the four beats.

X 1	X 2	X 3	X 4
When we smile at	someone,	we say,	"Welcome!"
When we frown at	someone,	we look	sad.
When we smile at	someone,	we say,	"Glad you came!"
When we frown at	someone,	we look	mad.
Smiles	or frowns,	smiles	or frowns—
One is	up, and the	other is	down.

New Verses to an Old Song

Try these new verses to the tune of "I've Got the Joy, Joy, Joy, Joy Down in My Heart."

I've got the joy of God no matter what, it's down in my heart,
Down in my heart, down in my heart.
I've got the joy of God no matter what, it's down in my heart—
Down in my heart to stay.

And now I'm smiling, smiling, smiling, smiling down in my heart,
Down in my heart, down in my heart.
And now I'm smiling, smiling, smiling, smiling down in my heart,
Down in my heart to stay.

Patience

Patience is definitely one virtue everyone needs! Let the children try the chants below to learn more about being patient.

Taking Turns

Divide the children into pairs and teach them this chant.

X	X	X	X	
1	2	3	4	
My turn,	your turn,	my turn,	your turn—	*(Hold hands and walk in a circle.)*
Each of	us must	wait some-	times.	*(Stand still.)*
My turn,	your turn,	my turn,	your turn—	*(Hold hands and walk in a circle.)*
We'll be	patient,	We'll be	kind.	*(Stand still.)*

Waiting

No matter how well you plan, sometimes you end up waiting with children who are at the age where waiting is a difficult task. Use this chant to fill a gap and to teach the children about patience.

A man's wisdom gives him patience; it is to his glory to overlook an offense. (Proverbs 19:11)

Hold up one hand and extend your index finger. "Wag" the finger back and forth like a pendulum on a clock as you say this rhyme with the children. Invite them to join you, even if just on the "tick-tock" lines.

1	2	3	4
Tick-	tock,	tick-	tock.
There are	times we	have to	wait,
Tick-	tock,	tick-	tock.
For one	minute	or a	few.
Tick-	tock,	tick-	tock,
There are	times we	have to	wait.
Tick-	tock,	tick-	tock.
I'll be	patient,	how about	you?

Patience

continued

Sometimes it is hard for children to keep their voices down. They must learn to be patient and control themselves in certain situations. The activity below is a perfect way to help them learn this.

Inside Voices, Outside Voices

Gather in a circle and demonstrate for the children an outside voice (not yelling, but speaking clearly and loudly) and an inside voice (not whispering, but speaking quietly and calmly). Use hand signals as well as voice changes to remind the children of the difference. When you are demonstrating an inside voice, use your index finger and thumb on one hand to show a small space to accompany your small voice. When you are demonstrating an outside voice, use both hands, palms facing each other, to show a bigger space. Have the children practice with you saying "outside voices" with their outside voice and "inside voices" with their inside voice.

Practice saying the rhythm chant below together. If the children are able to learn it, teach them the whole rhyme. If that seems like a bit much for them, just have them fill in the words in quotes as you prompt them with your hand signals.

X	X	X	X
1	2	3	4
When we're on the	inside,	"inside	voices."
When we're on the	outside,	"OUTSIDE	VOICES."
"OUTSIDE	VOICES,"	"inside	voices,"
We can	do them	both.	

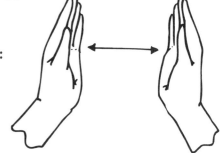

Change the chant a little to remind the children about another time to be quiet.

When we're in a	circle,	"inside	voices."
When we're on the	playground,	"OUTSIDE	VOICES."
"OUTSIDE	VOICES,"	"inside	voices"—
Which do	we use	now?	

You might also try some of these options with the chant above:

When we're in a	prayer time . . .
When we're at the	table . . .
When we're in the	hallway . . .

SS48843

Kindness

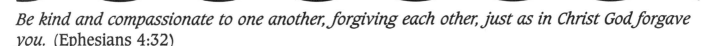

Be kind and compassionate to one another, forgiving each other, just as in Christ God forgave you. (Ephesians 4:32)

Please and Thank You

Use this song to remind the children to treat each other kindly. If you use this little song enough as you are working with the children at tables or in small groups, soon they will be able to sing it with you.

(Tune: "Frère Jacques")

"Please" and "Thank you,"
"Please" and "Thank you,"
Are kind words,
Are kind words.
Please will someone help me?
Please pass me a crayon.
Thank you, sir.
Thank you, sir.

You can substitute your own words for lines 5 and 6 to better relate to your specific situation.

Kind Person, Unkind Person

Use the finger puppets on page 64 to do the activity below and on page 64 about choices. When there is a question in the script, take time to let the children answer that question using their puppets.

This is a kind person. (*Show the positive-looking puppet now, and then again each time it is mentioned.*)

This is an unkind person. (*Show the negative-looking puppet now, and then each time it is mentioned.*)

A kind person likes to smile and say "Hi there," to the people he or she meets.

An unkind person doesn't smile. This person just looks down and walks by like he or she is angry.

Kindness

continued

Who would you rather say "hello" to, a kind person or an unkind person?

If you say "hi" to a kind person, what do you think this person will say back to you?

A kind person likes to help. When someone is lost, the kind person asks, "Can I help you?"
An unkind person doesn't like to help. When someone is lost, the unkind person doesn't help.

Who would you rather see when you need help, a kind person or an unkind person?

If you ask a kind person for help, what do you think this person would say?

A kind person has a friendly voice, and everyone likes to hear from this person.
An unkind person is a little gruff, and when he or she calls, it's a little scary.

Who would you rather talk to, a kind person or an unkind person?

If a kind person called you, how do you think this person would say "hello"?

A kind person does what the Bible says: "Be kind to each other."
An unkind person doesn't do what the Bible says: "Be kind to each other."

Who would you rather be, a kind person or an unkind person?

What are some ways you can be kind to someone?

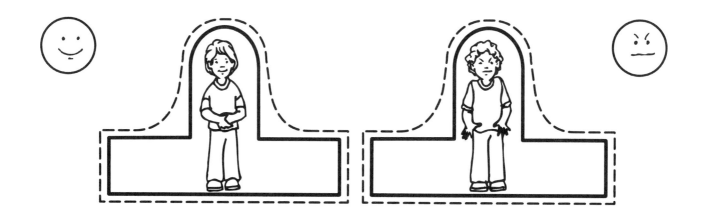

Secure with tape.

64

SS48843

Goodness

. . . do good, to be rich in good deeds, and to be generous and willing to share. (1 Timothy 6:18)

All children want to be good. Show them the way with the songs below and on page 66 and with the finger play on page 66.

Generosity

(Tune: "Gonna Lay Down My Burden, Down by the Riverside")

Gonna give what I can when
   (clap) somebody needs my help,
(clap) Somebody needs my help,
(clap) Somebody needs my help.
Gonna give what I can when
   (clap) somebody needs my help.
That's gen-er-os-i-ty.

Gonna share with my neighbor when
   (clap) we play together again,
(clap) We play together again,
(clap) We play together again.
Gonna share with my neighbor when
   (clap) we play together again.
That's gen-er-os-i-ty.

Gonna let someone else go first
   (clap) sometimes instead of me,
(clap) Sometimes instead of me,
(clap) Sometimes instead of me.
Gonna let someone else go first
   (clap) sometimes instead of me.
That's gen-er-os-i-ty.

Gonna help my mother (father) clean it up
   (clap) even if she (he) doesn't ask,
(clap) even if she (he) doesn't ask,
(clap) even if she (he) doesn't ask.
Gonna help my mother (father) clean it up
   (clap) even if she (he) doesn't ask.
That's gen-er-os-i-ty.

SS48843

Goodness

Tell the Truth

(Tune: "The Farmer in the Dell")

We need to tell the truth.
We need to tell the truth.
Because the Bible tells us so,
We need to tell the truth.

A Prayer for Goodness

Goodness means we want to do

Just what God has told us to.   *(Hold your hands out, palms up, as if you're reading the Bible.)*

Goodness means we treat each person with great respect.   *(Salute with your right hand.)*

Goodness means we wish good things

For all our friends and family.   *(Make big circles with both hands to show "all.")*

Goodness means we say our thanks for everything we get.   *(Place hands in front of you, palms up.)*

Fill our hearts with goodness, Lord.   *(Put hands together as in prayer.)*

Make us more like You.   *(Point up as if you are pointing to God.)*

Fill our hearts with goodness, Lord.   *(Put hands together as in prayer.)*

Make us more like You.   *(Point up as if you are pointing to God.)*

Gentleness

Let your gentleness be evident to all. The Lord is near. (Philippians 4:5)

Jesus was so gentle! What a wonderful example for all of us! The children can learn about gentleness with the song and march below.

Gentle Hands

(Tune: "Lullaby and Goodnight")

Gentle hands, gentle hands,
Touching softly and kindly,
Never hurting, never hurting,
Always loving and kind.

Gentle hands, gentle hands,
Being careful with each other,
Gentle hands, gentle hands,
Loving everyone we meet.

Walking Softly, Walking Loudly

You'll need rhythm sticks and a small drum or some kind of metronome to keep a steady beat as you walk around the circle in this rhythm march. Use this march to remind the children to use their inside behavior. It is a good activity to get some wiggles out before you gather in a circle.

1	2	3	4

(Take a step with each beat, quietly, on your tiptoes.)

Walk-	ing	soft-	ly,
Walk	ing	soft-	ly,
This is	how we	walk in-	side.

(Take a step with each beat, making a noise with each step.)

Walk-	ing	loud-	ly,
Walk-	ing	loud-	ly,
We can	walk this	way out-	side.
Out-	side,	out-	side.

(Take a step with each beat, quietly, on your tiptoes.)

| In- | side, | in- | side. |

(Say this line quietly as you sit in place.)

| Let's | sit | down. |

Forgiveness

(based on Matthew 18:21–35)

The Unforgiving Servant

One thing God wants all Christians to do is learn how to forgive those who harm us. Use the finger puppets and the song on page 69 to review this powerful story of forgiveness and to help the children learn to forgive others.

Puppets:

king (right index finger)
servant who owed $1,000 (left index finger)
friend who owed $100 (left thumb)

Jesus told a story to teach us about forgiving. He said that the kingdom of heaven is like a king (*show king*) and his servants. The king had a servant who owed him 1000 dollars. (*Show servant puppet.*)

The king went to that servant and said, "Pay me my money!" Since the man didn't have the money, he was going to lose everything he had.

The servant bowed before the king and begged him for forgiveness. (*Have the servant puppet bow.*) The king finally said, "OK. I'll forgive you for not paying me back this time. Go on your way." (*Hide the king puppet.*)

That servant was so happy. (*Servant puppet bounces along.*) He went on his way and then . . . (*servant stops suddenly*) he saw one of his friends who owed him just a hundred dollars. (*Show friend.*) Now a hundred dollars is a lot of money, but it is not as much as $1,000! The servant grabbed his friend and began to hurt him and said, "Pay back what you owe me!"

The friend bowed (*puppet bows*) before the servant and begged him for forgiveness. But the servant wouldn't forgive his friend. (*Move puppet back and forth to say "no."*) He had him thrown into prison! (*Hide friend puppet.*)

The king heard about this, and he was angry. (*Bring the king puppet back in.*) He said, "I can't believe I forgave you and then you didn't forgive your friend. I'm going to send you to jail after all!" (*Move king puppet angrily.*)

How sad for the servant! He had been forgiven. He should have learned to forgive. We should learn to forgive, too.

 SS48843

Forgiveness

continued

Use the song below to close your story.

God Forgave Our Sins

God for - gave our sins, so we for - give each oth - er.

God for - gave our sins, so we for - give each oth - er.

The Unforgiving Servant Puppet Patterns

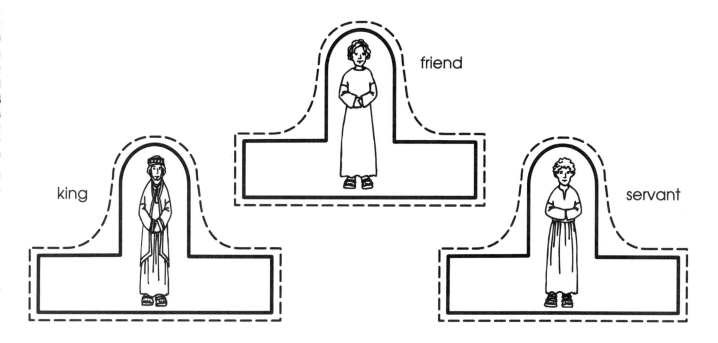

friend

king

servant

SS48843

The Golden Rule

(Matthew 7:12)

". . . do to others what you would have them do to you . . ." (Matthew 7:12)

Discuss the Golden Rule with the children. Then have the children sit in a circle on the floor, cross-legged, and teach them the song below and the one on page 71.

If We Want to Be Treated . . .

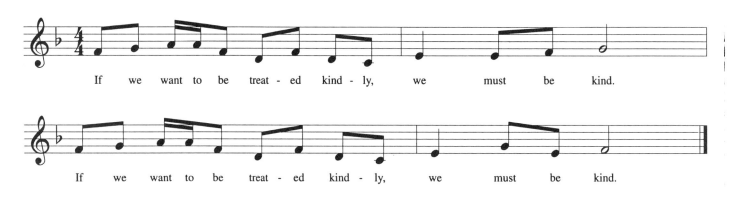

If we want to be treat - ed kind - ly, we must be kind.

If we want to be treat - ed kind - ly, we must be kind.

Add these verses and motions once the children are familiar with the tune.

If we want to be listened to, we must listen first. (*Put hand to ear.*)
If we want to be listened to, we must listen first.

If we want to play with toys, we must learn to share. (*Put hands out, palms up.*)
If we want to play with toys, we must learn to share.

If we want to be forgiven, we must forgive, we must forgive. (*Put hands across heart.*)
If we want to be forgiven, we must forgive, we must forgive.

Add in other verses and motions to make it a fun song. Examples: "If we want to hold a hand," "If we want to get a hug," etc. Allow the children to make up some verses of their own.

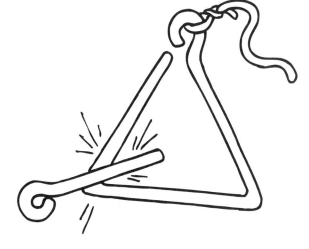

The Golden Rule

continued

This song is a wonderful way to remind the children of this very important rule.

Do Unto Others

Do un - to oth - ers as you would have them do

un - to you, un - to you.

Do un - to oth - ers as you would have them do

un - to you.

SS48843

The Fruit of the Spirit

(Galatians 5:22–23)

Discuss the fruit of the Spirit with the children. Talk about ways the children can show others how they have these fruits in their lives. Then sing the songs below and on page 73.

But the fruit of the Spirit is love, joy, peace, patience, kindness, goodness, faithfulness, gentleness and self-control. Against such things there is no law. (Galatians 5:22-23)

The Fruit of the Spirit

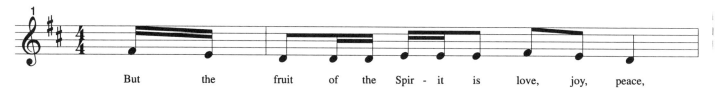

SS48843

The Fruit of the Spirit

continued

The Fruit Song

SS48843

Faith

(Hebrews 1 and 2)

Faith in God is something all Christians must have. Have the children stand in a circle, facing the center, as they sing this song. Discuss ways they show their faith in God. Then sing the songs below and on page 75.

We Have Faith

(Tune: "Three Blind Mice")

We have faith. We have faith.　　(*Point to yourself.*)

So we believe, so we believe,　　(*Put right hand over heart.*)

That God will do what He said He would,　　(*Put right hand in front of you, but a little to the right, palm up.*)

That He will help us do what we should,　　(*Put left hand in front of you, a little to the left, palm up.*)

And altogether we'll work for good,　　(*Have everyone hold hands, and then raise them as if in triumph.*)

For we have faith! We have faith!

Faith

continued

When We Have Faith

Now faith is be-ing sure of what we hope for and

cer-tain of what we can't see._____ Faith is be-ing sure of what

we hope for and cer-tain of what we can't see._____ When

we have faith, then we be-lieve that God's____ Word is

true._____ When we have faith, then we be-lieve that

God is help-ing me and you._____

SS48843

Love

(Matthew 22:37–39)

Love is such an important part of everyone's life. Teach the children how to love God. Have them sit in a circle, cross-legged. Then teach them this simple rhythm. They can also sing it using the tune below.

1	2	3	4
(clap on legs)	(clap hands)	(clap on legs)	(clap hands)

Once the children are familiar with the rhythm, teach them this verse:

1	2	3	4
Love the	Lord your	God	with
All	your	heart,	
All	your	soul,	
All	your	strength,	and
Love	your	neigh-	bor
as	your-	self.	

Love the Lord, Your God

Love the Lord your God with all your heart, all your soul,

all your strength; and love your neigh-bor as your-self.

SS48843

Love

continued

This song is perfect to use to remind the children to love one another.

We Know We Are God's Children

We know we are God's chil-dren when we love one an-oth-er,

love one an-oth-er, love one an-oth-er. We

know we are God's chil-dren when we love one an-oth-er,

just like Je-sus said.

77

SS48843

Prayers

Prayers of Petition

(to ask for something)

Help the children learn how to pray to ask for things by teaching them the prayer below and the song on page 80.

Prayer Request Rhyme

Have the children sit in a circle, cross-legged. Teach them this simple rhythm and chant.

1	2	3	4
(clap on legs)	*(clap on legs)*	*(clap hands)*	*(clap hands)*
Lord,	please	hear	
our	re-	quest.	
Thank	You,	God,	for
hear-		ing.	

Once the children are familiar with the chant, give each child a chance to offer a prayer request (without the rhythm). Respond and pray for each child's request by repeating this chant as a group but substituting the child's name for "our." For instance, "Lord please hear Heather's request. Thank You, God, for hearing."

When all the children who choose to have given a request, end with the chant (using "our" rather than a child's name) and add:

1	2	3	4
(clap on legs)	*(clap on legs)*	*(clap hands)*	*(clap hands)*
A-			
men.			

Prayers of Petition

continued

Teach the song below to the children. When they are familiar with it, add the motions (below).

Sometimes When We Pray

Some-times when we pray to God, we ask Him what to do. Some-times when we pray to God, we

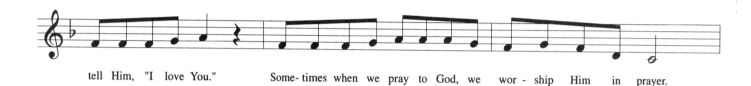

tell Him, "I love You." Some-times when we pray to God, we wor-ship Him in prayer.

Some-times when we pray to God, we say, "We're glad You're there." But some-times when we pray to God, we

need some-thing that day. And eve-ry time we pray to God, He lis-tens when we pray.

Sometimes when we pray to God, we ask Him what to do. (*Put hands out, palms up, in a shrug.*)

Sometimes when we pray to God, we tell Him, "I love You." (*Cross arms over chest in a hug.*)

Sometimes when we pray to God, we worship Him in prayer. (*Put palms together, as if in prayer.*)

Sometimes when we pray to God, we say, "We're glad You're there." (*Point up to God as if you're talking to Him.*)

But sometimes when we pray to God, we need something that day. (*Put hands in front of you, palms up, as if you're waiting to have something put in them.*)

And every time we pray to God, He listens when we pray. (*Put hand to ear as if you're listening.*)

SS48843

Prayers of Gratitude

(to thank God for something in particular)

The song below is a great way for the children to thank God for the many gifts He gives them.

We Thank You

(tune: "The Doxology")

We thank You for the gifts You send,

Our families and each new friend,

The clothes we wear, the food we eat,

We thank You, God, for everything. Amen.

We Are Grateful

Sit in a circle and clap to a steady rhythm as you pray this simple prayer. Allow the children to fill in the blanks. Take time to listen to the children tell you about the things in their lives that they are grateful for. If they need some hints, ask them about family, friends, pets, homes, or places. Rather than expecting them to speak their suggestions in rhythm, ask them before each verse what they would like to thank God for. Then you can say their suggestion as a group in that verse (like you might do in selecting new animals when you sing "Old MacDonald Had a Farm").

1	2	3	4
(clap hands)	(clap hands)	(clap hands)	(clap hands)
Thanks	God,	for the	things
You have	given	us.	
Thanks	God,	for the	things
You have	given	us.	
Thank You	for the	(flow-	ers).
Thank You	for the	(flow-	ers).
Thanks	God,	for the	things
You have	given	us.	

SS48843

Prayers of Gratitude

continued

Have the children stand in a circle as you teach them the song below that they can sing at any time. Then teach them the motions to go with it (below).

Thank-You Song

Thank You, God, for flowers that grow. Thank You, God, for pla - ces we go.

Thanks for things so good to eat. Thanks for new friends that we meet.

Thank You, we thank You, God.

Motions:

flowers that grow	*(Hold both hands so that your fingers are scrunched together; open them like a flower blooming.)*
places we go	*(Face toward the middle of the circle and stand still.)*
food to eat	*(Move hands and mouth as if eating.)*
friends that we meet	*(Hold hands in the circle.)*
last line	*(Still holding hands, swing your arms in and out of the circle.)*

Prayers of Worship

(to tell God how great He is)

The songs below are a great way for the children to express to God how wonderful He is!

We Worship You, God
(Tune: "I Love the Mountains")

We worship You God.
We know You care for us.
We know You're strong and will
Always be there for us.
Teach us to follow You,
And teach us to obey.
We will worship,
We will worship,
We will worship
You, O God.

We Worship You

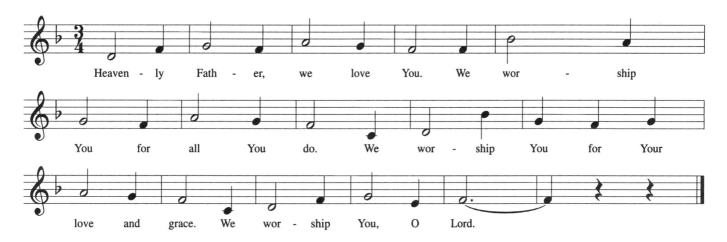

Heaven - ly Fath - er, we love You. We wor - ship You for all You do. We wor - ship You for Your love and grace. We wor - ship You, O Lord.

SS48843

Prayers of Communion

(Just to be with God)

This song will help the children learn to tell God that they love Him and want to live with Him.

Just to Be With You

Just   to   be   with   You,   O   Lord,

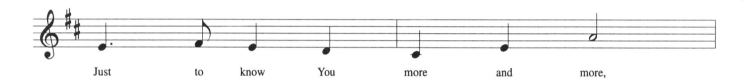

Just   to   know   You   more   and   more,

Just   to   tell   You   we   love   You,

That's   why   we   have   come.

SS48843

Prayers of Communion

God Is Always With Us

Celebrate spending time with God by doing the rhythm and movement march below. You'll need a small drum or rhythm sticks and someone to play a slow, steady beat. Before you begin, practice the motions with the children.

To begin, gather in a circle. Have someone slowly and rhythmically hit the drum. Have everyone join hands in a circle. Teach the children to walk in a circle, taking one step for each drum beat. Practice this before you add the movements.

Repeat this song with the children, leading them in the motions, until they can say it with you.

1	2	3	4	
God is	always	with	us.	(*Walk to the right.*)
Thank You,	God, for	being	here.	(*Face the middle on "here."*)
You are	with us	when we	sleep.	(*Place palms of hands together and put up to the side of the face like a pillow.*)
You are	with us	when we	play.	(*Clap hands to the beat.*)
You are	with us	every	day.	(*Cross arms over chest in a hug.*)
Thank	You,	God.		(*Point up as if you're pointing to God.*)

God Is There

(Tune: "If You're Happy and You Know It")

If we're walking down the street, God is there.
When we go somewhere to eat, God is there.
He has promised He would stay
Right beside us all the way.
So we thank You, God, for being here today.

If we're sitting in our house, God is there.
If we're quiet as a mouse, God is there.
He has promised He would stay
Right beside us all the way.
So we thank You, God, for being here today.

If we're swinging in a swing, God is there.
If we're playing anything, God is there.
He has promised He would stay
Right beside us all the way.
So we thank You, God, for being here today.

Prayers for Food

(table blessings)

The song below will help remind the children to be thankful for the wonderful food God gives them.

The Food's on the Table

The food's on the ta - ble, and

we're sit - ting 'round.

So we thank You,

Lord. We

take time to thank You, our

heads are bowed down.

We thank You,

Lord.

SS48843

Prayers to Open Class

The children will enjoy singing the songs below and on page 88 as they gather together each time they meet. These songs will remind them to start off their day by saying "hello" to God and singing praises to Him.

We Have Come

Heaven - ly Fath - er, we have come, Come to - geth - er on this day.

Teach us what we need to know. Help us to o - bey.

We Shake Hands

This action rhyme is a great way to get class started. Have the children stand in a circle.

We shake hands to say "hello."	*(Shake hands with the person to your right.)*
We're together to learn and grow.	*(Put hands together, palms in, and move them apart, to signify growing.)*
We shake hands to say "hello."	*(Shake hands with the person to your left.)*
Welcome here today.	*(Sit down in your place.)*

Prayers to Open Class

continued

Together Today

Spend - ing time to - geth - er, Lov - ing one an - oth - er,

Learn - ing what we need to grow clos - er to the Fath - er.

Lord, help us to hear You. Teach us how to pray.

Thank You that we get to be to - geth - er to - day.

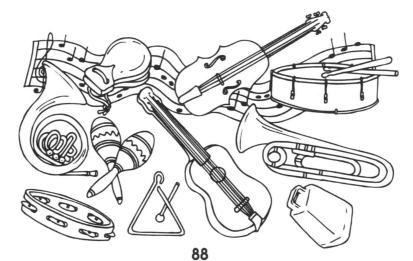

SS48843

Prayers to Close Class

The songs below and on page 90 are a nice way for the children to end their time together and to give praise to God.

Share His Love

Prayers to Close Class

continued

Help Us Grow

God has brought us here to - geth - er.

He'll be with us as we go.

Fath - er, help us love our neigh - bors.

Give us wis - dom, help us grow.

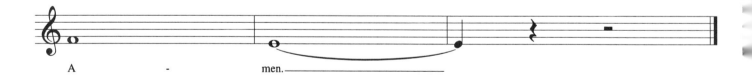

A - men.

Time to Say "Good-bye"

Have the children gather in a circle when it's almost time to leave class. Say the rhyme below together.

It's time we say "good-bye,"   (Wave your hand.)
And "Hope to see you soon!"   ("Wag" your index finger toward the middle of the group or point to friends.)

"It's been fun to be together."   (Put your hands on the shoulders of the people on your right and left.)

"God bless you!"   (Give someone a hug.)

90

SS48843

Prayers of Intercession

(to pray for others)

It is important that the children remember to pray for others. You can simply say this rhyme as a prayer, or use the melody at the bottom of the page and sing it. Go around the circle and let the children fill in the blanks with names of friends they would like to pray for.

Bless My Friend

Bless my friend _____.

Help him (her), Lord, I pray.

Bless my friend _____.

Help him (her) on his (her) way.

Bless My Friend

When singing the song below with the children, substitute names for "Samuel." Change "him/his" to "her" where appropriate.

Prayers of Intercession

continued

This song is perfect to sing to help the children learn to be a good friend and pray for their friends.

Praying Means You're Helping

When a friend of mine needs help, and I don't know what to do,——— I

give a hug and a great big smile, and say, "I'll pray for you."———

Then I go up in-to my room, and I shut my door be-hind,——— and

ask my Heav-en-ly Fa - ther to help this friend of mine.———

Chorus

Pray - ing means you're help - ing.——— Pray - ing is like be - ing there.———

Pray - ing means you're help - ing.——— Pray - ing means you care.———

SS48843

Prayers for Safety

Staying safe is very important for children. Teach them the songs below to help them learn to pray for their safety and the safety of others.

The Safety Prayer
(Tune: "The Doxology")

Lord, keep us safe now as we go

And bring us back together so

We'll learn to live for You each day

And love each other on the way. Amen.

Keep Us Safe
(Tune: "Three Blind Mice")

Keep us safe. Keep us safe,

Lord, in Your hands, Lord, in Your hands,

And give us wisdom to walk Your way.

We know You'll protect us both night and day.

We know we're Your children and so we pray,

Please keep us safe. Keep us safe.

SS48843

Prayers for Safety

continued

All children get scared. The song below will help them learn what to do when they are afraid.

When We Are Afraid

Chorus

When we are a-fraid, keep us safe, O Lord. When we are a-fraid, keep us

safe. When we are a-fraid, keep us safe, O Lord. When we are a-fraid, keep us

Fine

safe. When we are a-lone or it's dark at night,

Help us to re-mem-ber, it will be all right. Teach us how to trust You.

(Repeat Chorus)
D. C. al Fine

Teach us how to pray. Teach us that we're in Your arms and that's where we will stay.

     SS48843

Scripture Quick Reference

Index to Original Songs

Index to Puppet Finger Plays